FLOODS:
CAUSES AND EFFECTS

by Anne Winch

12
STORY LIBRARY
MORE TO EXPLORE

www.12StoryLibrary.com

12-Story Library is an imprint of Bookstaves.

Developed and produced for 12-Story Library by Focus Strategic Communications Inc.

Library of Congress Cataloging-in-Publication Data
Names: Winch, Anne, author.
Title: Floods : causes and effects / by Anne Winch.
Description: Mankato, MInnesota : 12-Story Library, [2022] | Series: Wild weather |
Includes bibliographical references and index. | Audience: Ages 10–13 | Audience: Grades 4–6
Identifiers: LCCN 2020017451 (print) | LCCN 2020017452 (ebook) | ISBN 9781645821472 (library binding) |
ISBN 9781645821854 (paperback) | ISBN 9781645822202 (pdf)
Subjects: LCSH: Floods—Juvenile literature.
Classification: LCC GB1399 .W53 2022 (print) | LCC GB1399 (ebook) | DDC 551.48/9—dc23
LC record available at https://lccn.loc.gov/2020017451
LC ebook record available at https://lccn.loc.gov/2020017452

About the Cover
Spring floods submerge a community.

Access free, up-to-date content on this topic plus a full digital version of this book. Scan the QR code on page 31 or use your school's login at 12StoryLibrary.com.

Table of Contents

A Lot of Water

A flood is a lot of water that is out of control. Water overflows and covers land that is normally dry. Floods can happen in many ways. Sometimes too much rain all at once can cause a flood. Lots of snow and ice that melts too fast can cause a flood. Sometimes a large storm can cause a flood on the seacoast. Even a beaver

Flood water is usually dirty.

SPEED LIMIT

Flooding makes driving impossible.

dam can cause a flood. Floods can be long-term events that happen over days or weeks. This gives people some time to prepare for it.

Floods are one of the most common natural disasters on Earth. They can cause a lot of damage to property.

Floods destroy crops, buildings, and wash away trees. Sometimes they wash away bridges, cars, houses, and even people. This makes them very dangerous.

2

Number of feet (0.6 m) of rushing water that will sweep a car away in a flood

- The most common type of flood is a river overflowing its banks.
- Just one inch (2.5 cm) of flood water can cause significant damage to property.
- In some areas, flooding provides a way to collect water to be used through the year to water crops.

Flash Floods Happen Fast

A flash flood is a rapid rise of fast-moving water. It is different from other floods. It usually happens in less than six hours. It is too fast for people to prepare for it. Flash floods can be caused by a sudden, heavy rainfall. Another cause is a dam breaking or an ice jam in a river.

The fast-moving waters in flash floods are dangerous. Rushing water can move

9

Number of feet (2.7 m) per second that fast water can move in a flash flood

- Flash floods can have walls of water as high as 20 feet (6 m).
- In Australia, flash floods are also known as overland flooding.
- A flash flood in Russia during the summer of 2012 has been connected to climate change.

Flash floods can quickly wash away roads.

rocks that weigh almost one hundred pounds (45 kg). The water in flash floods can carry all kinds of debris. This makes them even more dangerous. The moving debris causes injuries to people and damages buildings.

FLASH FLOOD DEATHS

Many deaths in flash floods happen in vehicles. Being in a vehicle is very dangerous during a flood. It is very difficult to judge how deep flood waters may be on a road. Just a foot of water will cause most vehicles to float.

Floods Happen Worldwide

Floodplains in the Netherlands.

Floods occur all over the world. Floods claim thousands of lives. They leave cities in ruins. Sometimes they even change the features of the land. Anywhere it rains, it could flood. River floodplains are one main area.

The sea coast is another. Long periods of heavy rainfall also create conditions for floods. Sometimes flooding happens when natural areas are destroyed. Cutting down forests leads to soil erosion. The soil flows into the rivers,

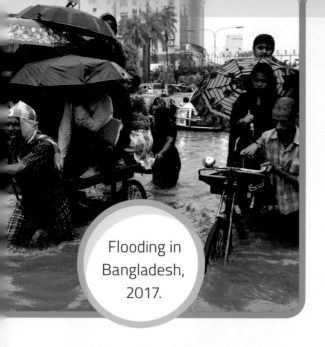

Flooding in Bangladesh, 2017.

21 million

Average number of people affected by river floods each year

- Water flows naturally from high areas to low areas.
- Climate change is increasing the risk of floods worldwide.
- There are about 100,000 miles (160,000 km) of levees on US rivers.

blocking them. Water backs up and overflows the river banks, causing a flood.

Bangladesh is the most likely country to flood. The main reason is heavy rainfall during monsoon season. The top six countries most at risk for river flooding are in Asia.

CHANGING LANDSCAPE

Changing the landscape adds to the risk of flooding. Building cities and towns changes the features of the land. The natural plants and soil are replaced with hard surfaces. The hard surfaces stop water from being absorbed into the ground. Instead, the water flows directly into streams and rivers, raising their water level.

Climate Change Increases the Risk of Floods

Climate change increases the risk of floods all over the world. Higher average temperatures create warmer air. Warmer air holds more moisture. This means more and heavier rainfall. The soil becomes too wet and cannot absorb any more water.

Heavy rainfall is a lot of rain all at once. If the soil is already soaked, the water runs off instead of being absorbed. This causes flooding.

Higher temperatures lead to melting ice on the poles and in glaciers. The melted ice flows into the oceans, raising the sea levels. Higher water levels and warmer air create more frequent and stronger storms. Stronger storms and high

Heavy rain causes rivers to rise.

winds create a storm surge. A storm surge is a high wall of water that is pushed onto the land. This is bad news for coastal towns because there is more chance of flooding.

24
Rise in feet (7.4 m) of global sea levels if all the ice in Greenland melted

- Extreme weather will happen more often and be more serious as the climate warms up.
- As sea ice melts in the Arctic, animals such as walruses are losing their habitat.
- Water evaporation from the oceans is increasing as the average global temperature gets higher.

Flood Prediction is Challenging

Scientists can track storms, but it's difficult to predict how bad flooding will be.

A flood is one of the worst types of natural disasters. Predicting a flood is very tricky. Scientists use a lot of tools to predict floods. Some of these tools are satellites, lasers, and weather radar. The lasers are attached to airplanes. They scan shorelines to check for changes. Weather radar shows where rain is falling.

A lot of information is needed to predict floods. Scientists look at rainfall, soil moisture, and melting snow. Scientists use information to tell when the ground is dry or wet. When the ground is wet, it cannot soak up any more water. A flood is more likely to happen when the ground is already very wet.

Scientists collect dirt samples to check how wet the ground is.

THINK ABOUT IT

Deserts can also have serious flash floods. Why do you think floods can happen in a dry desert?

8.6 million
Number of Americans who live in an area in danger of coastal floods due to storm surges

- Floods kill more people in the US than hurricanes, tornadoes, or lightning.
- Scientists can usually tell if the weather conditions are right for a flash flood to occur.
- Researchers warn that risks of flooding are expected to increase in the future with climate change.

Flood Cleanup Is a Big Job

Flooding can cause problems for entire towns.

Damage from a flood affects every part of people's lives. Thousands of people are forced to leave their homes. Flooded workplaces mean people cannot work.

After a flood, everything is covered in mud and silt.

Removing mud is a big job. You might need a shovel to get a lot of it out. You have to use a hose to wash out of the

Belongings might need to be replaced after a flood.

rest of it. Everything needs to be scrubbed with hot water, soap, and disinfectant. After a good cleaning, the buildings must dry out completely to prevent mold. This could take weeks. Recovering from a flood takes a long time.

South Ferry Subway Station 1

8 million

Amount of household garbage in cubic yards (6 million cubic meters) that was created in Houston, TX, by Hurricane Harvey flooding in 2017

- That would fill the Houston Texan's stadium twice.
- In 1972, the coal mine dam in Buffalo Creek, West Virginia, burst. It poured water, coal sludge, and mud over the area and destroyed hundreds of homes.
- It took almost five years to reopen the South Ferry subway station in New York after it was flooded by Superstorm Sandy in 2012.

15

Floods Affect Wildlife, Too

During a flood, many people have to leave their homes. Animals also have to get away from flood waters. Wild animals are forced out of their homes. Animals such as deer and rabbits cannot live in water. They may need to travel a long way to find food and shelter away from the flood. These animals search for

higher ground. Sometimes people may find them looking for shelter in their backyards.

Some animals can escape the flood, but other animals get trapped in their homes. Groundhogs and moles live in tunnels underground. The tunnels get flooded, and the animals cannot escape. Some small mammals and birds

Even animals that love water can be displaced by floods.

can find safety high in the trees. Luckily, most animals are able to survive floods. Many of them find their way back to their homes, or they go to another area to make new homes.

THINK ABOUT IT

What might animals do to survive floods?

600,000

Estimated number of animals displaced by the flooding in Hurricane Katrina in 2005

- Animal care shelters are set up to take care of displaced pets.
- Many people use social media to help them find their pets after a flood.
- Thousands of farm animals died during a flood in Nebraska and Iowa in 2019.

8

There Can Be a Good Side to Floods

Watch out, a flood is coming. People often think of floods as scary disasters. They can be huge problems for people. In cities, floods can do a lot of damage. They cost a lot of money.

But floods are not all bad. Flooding has a positive impact for nature. Flood waters carry silt. Silt is made up of tiny particles of rocks and minerals. Silt helps the soil become more fertile. This benefits the soil and improves plant growth. This means it is really good for growing crops.

Floods also replace groundwater and surface water. This helps animals and humans.

18

$10 billion to $25 billion

Cost of floods each year in the US

- Areas that have been changed a lot by people are more affected by floods than natural, wild areas are.
- Floods can provide fish and other water animals with temporary areas to lay eggs and get food.
- Some birds breed when it floods.

Animals may find more drinking water from flooding.

THE ROLE OF WETLANDS

Wetlands are swampy or marshy areas that are very important. Floods help wetlands. They replace surface water and fill dried out marshes. Wetlands protect and improve water quality. They store water during dry seasons. Wetlands also provide habitats for fish and wildlife. They are used by water birds for nesting and breeding.

9

Training is Important for Flood Rescue

Boats are often the only way to get around after a flood.

Rescuing flood victims is a tough job. Many rescuers are paid first responders. Other are volunteers with special training.

20 It's important for rescuers to know how

to rescue people safely. They learn about how water moves. They learn how to move a boat through city streets.

Rescuers check the water carefully. They look for objects hidden under the surface.

64
Number of pets rescued by a trucker in South Carolina after Hurricane Florence in 2018

- Emergency Animal Rescue Shelter, also known as "Noah's Ark," is run out of a bus to take animals to shelters.
- Animal Rescue Network finds and rescues pets in flooded areas.
- One man personally rescued more than 400 people after Hurricane Katrina in 2005.

Sometimes rescuers have to do first aid. They also need to know rope skills such as knot tying.

RESCUE TACTICS

Rescue boats hold only three or four passengers plus the crew. They check for people in the most need. Rescue teams take the very old, very young, and injured people to safety first. One person on the boat is a spotter. Spotters check for people who might have fallen into the water. The spotter watches them until they are rescued.

The Dangers of Flood Water

Flood water is not for drinking.

Floods do more than just damage property. A big danger is what is in the flood water. Bacteria, gas and oil, and sewage end up in flood water. Rescue boats leak oil and gas into the water. Garbage gets swept up in the water, too. Sewer systems overflow, dumping raw sewage into the flood waters. Pipes in people's homes back up, making toilets and drains overflow. These cause serious health hazards to people caught in a flood.

You could get an infection if contaminated water gets in your mouth or eyes. Contaminated drinking water is the biggest cause of infection. Eating or drinking anything touched by flood water can cause health problems. Washing in contaminated water is also unsafe. Only boiled water is safe to drink or use to wash.

There are other dangers when water floods an area. Mosquitoes like to breed in still water. Flood waters attract mosquitoes. Mosquitoes carry diseases such as malaria and West Nile virus.

3,000
Number of different types of mosquitoes in the world

- All types of mosquitoes need water to breed.
- Climate change may increase the number of mosquitoes there are in the world.
- Mosquitoes usually make their appearance about two weeks after a flood.

Famous Floods Around the World

Flooding in China, 1931.

Flood disasters have occurred all through history. The first recorded flood was in the Netherlands in 838. A storm surge broke the dikes and flooded the land. In 1931, there was incredible flooding in central China. Three major rivers flooded. Thousands drowned. Others died of starvation and disease after the flood.

In 1841, the Indus River in South Asia was dammed by a huge landslide. An enormous lake formed. Then the dam burst. A flood wave raced down the valley. It destroyed whole villages.

In 1966, a huge flood swept through Florence, Italy. Water, mud, and sewage destroyed homes, businesses, art galleries, and libraries. Water reached 20 feet (6 m) in parts of the city.

Flooding in Florence, Italy, 1966.

THINK ABOUT IT

If you were in charge of an area that has many floods, what would you do?

4 million

Approximate number of people who died because of the 1931 floods in China

- The Indus river flood wave was almost 100 feet (30 m) high.
- More than 1 million books were soaked and covered with mud in Florence's National Central Library.
- Young people from around the world came to Florence to help find paintings and books in the debris. They were called Mud Angels.

A Sinking New Orleans

New Orleans.

New Orleans is sinking a little at a time. Today much of the New Orleans area is more than 6 feet (2 m) below sea level. This makes storm surges and flooding very dangerous.

Flooding can damage bridges and other structures.

99 million
Average number of people affected by floods each year

- Underwater earthquakes can cause tidal waves. These can flood coastal towns.
- Flooding is one of the biggest threats from hurricanes.
- A few weeks after Katrina, Hurricane Rita damaged dozens more oil rigs.

New Orleans development has changed the wetlands and islands. Wetlands and islands can be barriers to storm surges. New Orleans' barriers are disappearing.

In 2005, Hurricane Katrina hit the Gulf Coast of the US. The storm surge broke the levees and flood walls protecting New Orleans. Water flooded the city. Hundreds of thousands of people had to leave their homes.

OIL RIGS ARE AT RISK IN HURRICANES

Oil rigs are large structures that are used to find and collect oil under the ocean. Huge waves from Hurricane Katrina flooded and destroyed many platforms. People live and work on the platforms. They can be hurt or killed. Damaged platforms can lead to oil leaks into the ocean.

Staying Safe in a Flood

Here are some ways to keep yourself and your family safe in a flood.

- Make a flood survival plan.

- Pick a meeting spot in case you have to leave your home.

Make sure everyone in the family knows where it is.

- Make sure cell phones are always charged for communication. Text messages are more reliable in an emergency.

FLOOD
SAFETY TIPS

BEFORE

STAY INFORMED ON LOCAL NEWS	PREPARE AN EMERGENCY BAG WITH FOOD, DRUGS, DOCUMENTS, FLASHLIGHT, PET ITEMS	KNOW HOW TO EVACUATE AND SAFE ALTERNATIVE ROUTES	LEAVE BEFORE FLOODING STARTS	IN FLOOD PRONE AREAS: KEEP USEFUL ITEMS AT HOME (SANDBAGS, LADDER, ROPE...)

DURING THE FLOOD

DISCONNECT ELECTRICITY AND GAS	DON'T WALK OR DRIVE IN FLOOD WATER	GET TO A HIGHER GROUND	FOLLOW EVACUATION ORDERS	FREE CATTLE AND LEAD ANIMALS TO A SAFER PLACE

AFTER

AVOID CONTACT WITH FLOOD WATER AND SWIMMING	DON'T TOUCH POWER LINES	DON'T GO HOME OR TO DISASTER AREAS UNTIL IT IS DECLARED SAFE	COMMUNICATE TO YOUR FAMILY THAT YOU ARE SAFE	WHEN BACK HOME: CLEAN AND DISINFECT SURFACES AND ITEMS

- Have an emergency survival kit. Your kit should include enough food and water for three days. Also include a first aid kit and medical supplies. Put in a complete change of clothes. Make copies of personal identification papers.

- If you have to leave your house, take your emergency kit and go. Leave everything else behind. Head to your meeting spot or the nearest shelter.

IMPORTANT DOCUMENTS

FIRST AID +

Glossary

bacteria
Tiny, one-celled living things found everywhere that can be helpful or harmful.

debris
All the bits of broken waste and damaged material left after a flood.

disinfectant
A chemical used to slow or stop germs by destroying bacteria.

displace
To cause something or someone to move from its proper place or home by a disaster such as extreme weather or war.

erosion
The wearing away of land, rock, and other materials by wind or water.

first responders
People who have special training and arrive first at an accident or disaster such as a flood.

floodplain
Low-lying ground near a river or stream that is easily flooded.

groundwater
Water that is beneath Earth's surface, held underground in the soil or rock crevices.

levee
A bank or wall built up with sand bags and other materials to prevent a river from flooding.

monsoon
A strong seasonal wind in southern Asia that may bring heavy rain.

sewage
The solid and liquid waste matter produced by a community.

Read More

Cosgrove, Brian. *Weather: Discover the World's Weather from Heat Waves and Droughts to Blizzards and Flood.* New York, NY: DK Eyewitness, 2016.

Johnson, Robin. *What Is a Flood?* New York, NY: Crabtree, 2016.

Normandeau, Sheryl. *Floods.* Collingwood, ON: Beech Street Books, 2019.

Portman, Michael. *Deadly Floods.* New York, NY: Gareth Stevens, 2012.

Visit 12StoryLibrary.com

Scan the code or use your school's login at **12StoryLibrary.com** for recent updates about this topic and a full digital version of this book. Enjoy free access to:

- Digital ebook
- Breaking news updates
- Live content feeds
- Videos, interactive maps, and graphics
- Additional web resources

Note to educators: Visit 12StoryLibrary.com/register to sign up for free premium website access. Enjoy live content plus a full digital version of every 12-Story Library book you own for every student at your school.

Index

About the Author

Anne Winch is an elementary school teacher in Barrie, Ontario. She lives with her husband and two Doodle puppies just north of Barrie. She is an avid reader, writer, and lifelong learner. She has finally found a way to incorporate all of these passions.

READ MORE FROM 12-STORY LIBRARY

Every 12-Story Library Book is available in many formats. For more information, visit **12StoryLibrary.com**